BLOG POST PLANNER

Name :

Address:

Phone:

Email:

BLOG POST PLANNER

Publish Date _______________

Category _______________

Title _______________

Call to Action _______________

Type

☐ Tutorial   ☐ List

☐ Review   ☐ Guest Post

Post status

○ Draft

○ Scheduled

○ Published

○ Edit

○ SEO

Keyword	Tags

Content

Checklist

○ _______________

○ _______________

○ _______________

○ _______________

○ _______________

○ _______________

○ _______________

○ _______________

○ _______________

○ _______________

○ _______________

Resources

Social Media

○

○

○

○

○

BLOG POST PLANNER

Publish Date ....

Category ....

Title ....

Call to Action ....

Type

- ☐ Tutorial
- ☐ Review
- ☐ List
- ☐ Guest Post

Post status

- ○ Draft
- ○ Scheduled
- ○ Published
- ○ Edit
- ○ SEO

Keyword	Tags

Checklist

- ○ ________________
- ○ ________________
- ○ ________________
- ○ ________________
- ○ ________________
- ○ ________________
- ○ ________________
- ○ ________________
- ○ ________________
- ○ ________________
- ○ ________________

Content

Resources

Social Media

- ○
- ○
- ○
- ○
- ○

BLOG POST PLANNER

Publish Date ....

Category ....

Title ....

Call to Action ....

Type

- [ ] Tutorial
- [ ] Review
- [ ] List
- [ ] Guest Post

Post status

- ○ Draft
- ○ Scheduled
- ○ Published
- ○ Edit
- ○ SEO

Keyword	Tags

Checklist

- ○ ——————————
- ○ ——————————
- ○ ——————————
- ○ ——————————
- ○ ——————————
- ○ ——————————
- ○ ——————————
- ○ ——————————
- ○ ——————————
- ○ ——————————
- ○ ——————————

Content

....

....

....

....

Resources

Social Media

- ○
- ○
- ○
- ○
- ○

BLOG POST PLANNER

Publish Date

Category

Title

Call to Action

Type

- ☐ Tutorial
- ☐ Review
- ☐ List
- ☐ Guest Post

Post status

- ○ Draft
- ○ Scheduled
- ○ Published
- ○ Edit
- ○ SEO

Keyword	Tags

Content

Checklist

Resources

Social Media

BLOG POST PLANNER

Publish Date

Category

Title

Call to Action

Type

☐ Tutorial   ☐ List
☐ Review   ☐ Guest Post

Post status

○ Draft

○ Scheduled

○ Published

○ Edit

○ SEO

Keyword	Tags

Checklist

○ ───────────
○ ───────────
○ ───────────
○ ───────────
○ ───────────
○ ───────────
○ ───────────
○ ───────────
○ ───────────
○ ───────────
○ ───────────

Content

Resources

Social Media

○
○
○
○
○

BLOG POST PLANNER

Publish Date

Category

Title

Call to Action

Type

☐ Tutorial   ☐ List

☐ Review   ☐ Guest Post

Post status

○ Draft

○ Scheduled

○ Published

○ Edit

○ SEO

Keyword	Tags

Checklist

○ ——————————
○ ——————————
○ ——————————
○ ——————————
○ ——————————
○ ——————————
○ ——————————
○ ——————————
○ ——————————
○ ——————————
○ ——————————

Content

Resources

Social Media

○
○
○
○
○

BLOG POST PLANNER

Publish Date ....

Category ....

Title ....

Call to Action ....

....

Type

☐ Tutorial   ☐ List
☐ Review   ☐ Guest Post

Post status

- ○ Draft
- ○ Scheduled
- ○ Published
- ○ Edit
- ○ SEO

Keyword	Tags

Content ....

....

....

....

Checklist

- ○ ______________________
- ○ ______________________
- ○ ______________________
- ○ ______________________
- ○ ______________________
- ○ ______________________
- ○ ______________________
- ○ ______________________
- ○ ______________________
- ○ ______________________
- ○ ______________________

Resources

Social Media

- ○
- ○
- ○
- ○
- ○

BLOG POST PLANNER

Publish Date

Category

Title

Call to Action

Type

- ☐ Tutorial
- ☐ Review
- ☐ List
- ☐ Guest Post

Post status

- ○ Draft
- ○ Scheduled
- ○ Published
- ○ Edit
- ○ SEO

Keyword	Tags

Content

Checklist

- ○
- ○
- ○
- ○
- ○
- ○
- ○
- ○
- ○
- ○
- ○

Resources

Social Media

- ○
- ○
- ○
- ○
- ○

BLOG POST PLANNER

Publish Date

Category

Title

Call to Action

Type

- ☐ Tutorial
- ☐ Review
- ☐ List
- ☐ Guest Post

Post status

- ○ Draft
- ○ Scheduled
- ○ Published
- ○ Edit
- ○ SEO

Keyword	Tags

Checklist

- ○
- ○
- ○
- ○
- ○
- ○
- ○
- ○
- ○
- ○
- ○

Content

Resources

Social Media

- ○
- ○
- ○
- ○
- ○

BLOG POST PLANNER

Publish Date ....

Category ....

Title ....

Call to Action ....

....

Type

- ☐ Tutorial
- ☐ Review
- ☐ List
- ☐ Guest Post

Post status

- ○ Draft
- ○ Scheduled
- ○ Published
- ○ Edit
- ○ SEO

Keyword	Tags

Checklist

- ○ ___________________
- ○ ___________________
- ○ ___________________
- ○ ___________________
- ○ ___________________
- ○ ___________________
- ○ ___________________
- ○ ___________________
- ○ ___________________
- ○ ___________________
- ○ ___________________

Content

....

....

....

Resources

Social Media

- ○
- ○
- ○
- ○
- ○

BLOG POST PLANNER

Publish Date _______________

Category _______________

Title _______________

Call to Action _______________
____

Type

☐ Tutorial ☐ List
☐ Review ☐ Guest Post

Keyword	Tags

Content
____
____
____

Post status

○ Draft
○ Scheduled
○ Published
○ Edit
○ SEO

Checklist

○ _______________
○ _______________
○ _______________
○ _______________
○ _______________
○ _______________
○ _______________
○ _______________
○ _______________
○ _______________

Resources

Social Media

○
○
○
○
○

BLOG POST PLANNER

Publish Date

Category

Title

Call to Action

Type

- ☐ Tutorial
- ☐ Review
- ☐ List
- ☐ Guest Post

Post status

- ○ Draft
- ○ Scheduled
- ○ Published
- ○ Edit
- ○ SEO

Keyword	Tags

Checklist

Content

Resources

Social Media

BLOG POST PLANNER

Publish Date

Category

Title

Call to Action

Type

- [ ] Tutorial
- [ ] Review
- [ ] List
- [ ] Guest Post

Post status

- ○ Draft
- ○ Scheduled
- ○ Published
- ○ Edit
- ○ SEO

Keyword	Tags

Content

Checklist

- ○
- ○
- ○
- ○
- ○
- ○
- ○
- ○
- ○
- ○
- ○

Resources

Social Media

- ○
- ○
- ○
- ○
- ○

BLOG POST PLANNER

Publish Date

Category

Title

Call to Action

Type

☐ Tutorial ☐ List

☐ Review ☐ Guest Post

Post status

○ Draft

○ Scheduled

○ Published

○ Edit

○ SEO

Keyword	Tags

Checklist

○ ___________
○ ___________
○ ___________
○ ___________
○ ___________
○ ___________
○ ___________
○ ___________
○ ___________
○ ___________
○ ___________

Content

Resources

Social Media

○
○
○
○
○

BLOG POST PLANNER

Publish Date ....

Category ....

Title ....

Call to Action ....

....

Type

☐ Tutorial   ☐ List

☐ Review   ☐ Guest Post

Post status

○ Draft

○ Scheduled

○ Published

○ Edit

○ SEO

Keyword	Tags

Content

Checklist

○ —————————————
○ —————————————
○ —————————————
○ —————————————
○ —————————————
○ —————————————
○ —————————————
○ —————————————
○ —————————————
○ —————————————

Resources

Social Media

○

○

○

○

○

BLOG POST PLANNER

Publish Date

Category

Title

Call to Action

Type

- ☐ Tutorial
- ☐ Review
- ☐ List
- ☐ Guest Post

Post status

- ○ Draft
- ○ Scheduled
- ○ Published
- ○ Edit
- ○ SEO

Keyword	Tags

Content

Checklist

- ○
- ○
- ○
- ○
- ○
- ○
- ○
- ○
- ○
- ○
- ○

Resources

Social Media

- ○
- ○
- ○
- ○
- ○

BLOG POST PLANNER

Publish Date

Category

Title

Call to Action

Type

- [ ] Tutorial
- [ ] Review
- [ ] List
- [ ] Guest Post

Post status

- ○ Draft
- ○ Scheduled
- ○ Published
- ○ Edit
- ○ SEO

Keyword	Tags

Content

Checklist

- ○
- ○
- ○
- ○
- ○
- ○
- ○
- ○
- ○
- ○
- ○

Resources

Social Media

- ○
- ○
- ○
- ○
- ○

BLOG POST PLANNER

Publish Date

Category

Title

Call to Action

Type

- ☐ Tutorial
- ☐ Review
- ☐ List
- ☐ Guest Post

Post status

- ○ Draft
- ○ Scheduled
- ○ Published
- ○ Edit
- ○ SEO

Keyword	Tags

Checklist

- ○ —————————
- ○ —————————
- ○ —————————
- ○ —————————
- ○ —————————
- ○ —————————
- ○ —————————
- ○ —————————
- ○ —————————
- ○ —————————
- ○ —————————

Content

Resources

Social Media

- ○
- ○
- ○
- ○
- ○

BLOG POST PLANNER

Publish Date

Category

Title

Call to Action

Type

- [ ] Tutorial
- [ ] Review
- [ ] List
- [ ] Guest Post

Post status

- ○ Draft
- ○ Scheduled
- ○ Published
- ○ Edit
- ○ SEO

Keyword	Tags

Checklist

Content

Resources

Social Media

BLOG POST PLANNER

Publish Date

Category

Title

Call to Action

Type

- ☐ Tutorial
- ☐ Review
- ☐ List
- ☐ Guest Post

Post status

- ○ Draft
- ○ Scheduled
- ○ Published
- ○ Edit
- ○ SEO

Keyword	Tags

Checklist

- ○ ——————————
- ○ ——————————
- ○ ——————————
- ○ ——————————
- ○ ——————————
- ○ ——————————
- ○ ——————————
- ○ ——————————
- ○ ——————————
- ○ ——————————
- ○ ——————————

Content

Resources

Social Media

- ○
- ○
- ○
- ○
- ○

BLOG POST PLANNER

Publish Date

Category

Title

Call to Action

Type

☐ Tutorial ☐ List

☐ Review ☐ Guest Post

Post status

○ Draft

○ Scheduled

○ Published

○ Edit

○ SEO

Keyword	Tags

Checklist

○ ────────────

○ ────────────

○ ────────────

○ ────────────

○ ────────────

○ ────────────

○ ────────────

○ ────────────

○ ────────────

○ ────────────

○ ────────────

Content

Resources

Social Media

○

○

○

○

○

BLOG POST PLANNER

Publish Date

Category

Title

Call to Action

Type

☐ Tutorial   ☐ List
☐ Review   ☐ Guest Post

Post status

○ Draft

○ Scheduled

○ Published

○ Edit

○ SEO

Keyword	Tags

Checklist

○ ——————————
○ ——————————
○ ——————————
○ ——————————
○ ——————————
○ ——————————
○ ——————————
○ ——————————
○ ——————————
○ ——————————
○ ——————————

Content

Resources

Social Media

○
○
○
○
○

BLOG POST PLANNER

Publish Date ....

Category ....

Title ....

Call to Action ....

Type

- ☐ Tutorial
- ☐ Review
- ☐ List
- ☐ Guest Post

Post status

- ○ Draft
- ○ Scheduled
- ○ Published
- ○ Edit
- ○ SEO

Keyword	Tags

Content

Checklist

- ○ ——————————
- ○ ——————————
- ○ ——————————
- ○ ——————————
- ○ ——————————
- ○ ——————————
- ○ ——————————
- ○ ——————————
- ○ ——————————
- ○ ——————————

Resources

Social Media

- ○
- ○
- ○
- ○
- ○

BLOG POST PLANNER

Publish Date

Category

Title

Call to Action

Type

☐ Tutorial   ☐ List

☐ Review   ☐ Guest Post

Post status

○ Draft

○ Scheduled

○ Published

○ Edit

○ SEO

Keyword	Tags

Checklist

○ _________________
○ _________________
○ _________________
○ _________________
○ _________________
○ _________________
○ _________________
○ _________________
○ _________________
○ _________________
○ _________________

Content

Resources

Social Media

○

○

○

○

○

BLOG POST PLANNER

Publish Date

Category

Title

Call to Action

Type

- ☐ Tutorial
- ☐ Review
- ☐ List
- ☐ Guest Post

Post status

- ○ Draft
- ○ Scheduled
- ○ Published
- ○ Edit
- ○ SEO

Keyword	Tags

Content

Checklist

- ○
- ○
- ○
- ○
- ○
- ○
- ○
- ○
- ○
- ○
- ○

Resources

Social Media

- ○
- ○
- ○
- ○
- ○

BLOG POST PLANNER

Publish Date

Category

Title

Call to Action

Type

☐ Tutorial ☐ List
☐ Review ☐ Guest Post

Post status

○ Draft

○ Scheduled

○ Published

○ Edit

○ SEO

Keyword	Tags

Checklist

○
○
○
○
○
○
○
○
○
○
○

Content

Resources

Social Media

○
○
○
○
○

BLOG POST PLANNER

Publish Date

Category

Title

Call to Action

Type

- ☐ Tutorial
- ☐ Review
- ☐ List
- ☐ Guest Post

Post status

- ○ Draft
- ○ Scheduled
- ○ Published
- ○ Edit
- ○ SEO

Keyword	Tags

Content

Checklist

- ○ ────────────
- ○ ────────────
- ○ ────────────
- ○ ────────────
- ○ ────────────
- ○ ────────────
- ○ ────────────
- ○ ────────────
- ○ ────────────
- ○ ────────────
- ○ ────────────

Resources

Social Media

- ○
- ○
- ○
- ○
- ○

BLOG POST PLANNER

Publish Date ....

Category ....

Title ....

Call to Action ....
....

Type

- ☐ Tutorial
- ☐ Review
- ☐ List
- ☐ Guest Post

Post status

- ○ Draft
- ○ Scheduled
- ○ Published
- ○ Edit
- ○ SEO

Keyword	Tags

Content

Checklist

Resources

Social Media

BLOG POST PLANNER

Publish Date

Category

Title

Call to Action

Type

☐ Tutorial   ☐ List

☐ Review   ☐ Guest Post

Post status

○ Draft

○ Scheduled

○ Published

○ Edit

○ SEO

Keyword	Tags

Content

Checklist

○ —
○ —
○ —
○ —
○ —
○ —
○ —
○ —
○ —
○ —
○ —

Resources

Social Media

○
○
○
○
○

BLOG POST PLANNER

Publish Date

Category

Title

Call to Action

Type

- ☐ Tutorial
- ☐ Review
- ☐ List
- ☐ Guest Post

Post status

- ○ Draft
- ○ Scheduled
- ○ Published
- ○ Edit
- ○ SEO

Keyword	Tags

Content

Checklist

Resources

Social Media

BLOG POST PLANNER

Publish Date ______________

Category ______________

Title ______________

Call to Action ______________

____

Type

☐ Tutorial   ☐ List

☐ Review   ☐ Guest Post

Post status

○ Draft

○ Scheduled

○ Published

○ Edit

○ SEO

Keyword	Tags

Checklist

○ ______________

○ ______________

○ ______________

○ ______________

○ ______________

○ ______________

○ ______________

○ ______________

○ ______________

○ ______________

○ ______________

Content

____

____

____

Resources

Social Media

○

○

○

○

○

BLOG POST PLANNER

Publish Date ....

Category ....

Title ....

Call to Action ....

....

Type

☐ Tutorial   ☐ List

☐ Review   ☐ Guest Post

Post status

○ Draft

○ Scheduled

○ Published

○ Edit

○ SEO

Keyword	Tags

Content ....

....

....

....

Checklist

○ ─────────────────
○ ─────────────────
○ ─────────────────
○ ─────────────────
○ ─────────────────
○ ─────────────────
○ ─────────────────
○ ─────────────────
○ ─────────────────
○ ─────────────────
○ ─────────────────

Resources

Social Media

○
○
○
○
○

BLOG POST PLANNER

Publish Date ....

Category ....

Title ....

Call to Action ....

....

Type

- ☐ Tutorial
- ☐ Review
- ☐ List
- ☐ Guest Post

Post status

- ○ Draft
- ○ Scheduled
- ○ Published
- ○ Edit
- ○ SEO

Keyword	Tags

Checklist

- ○ ______________
- ○ ______________
- ○ ______________
- ○ ______________
- ○ ______________
- ○ ______________
- ○ ______________
- ○ ______________
- ○ ______________
- ○ ______________

Content

....

....

....

....

Resources

Social Media

- ○
- ○
- ○
- ○
- ○

BLOG POST PLANNER

Publish Date

Category

Title

Call to Action

Type

- [ ] Tutorial
- [ ] Review
- [ ] List
- [ ] Guest Post

Post status

- O Draft
- O Scheduled
- O Published
- O Edit
- O SEO

Keyword	Tags

Checklist

Content

Resources

Social Media

BLOG POST PLANNER

Publish Date

Category

Title

Call to Action

Type

- ☐ Tutorial
- ☐ Review
- ☐ List
- ☐ Guest Post

Post status

- ○ Draft
- ○ Scheduled
- ○ Published
- ○ Edit
- ○ SEO

Keyword	Tags

Checklist

- ○
- ○
- ○
- ○
- ○
- ○
- ○
- ○
- ○
- ○
- ○

Content

Resources

Social Media

- ○
- ○
- ○
- ○
- ○

BLOG POST PLANNER

Publish Date

Category

Title

Call to Action

Type

☐ Tutorial   ☐ List

☐ Review   ☐ Guest Post

Post status

○ Draft

○ Scheduled

○ Published

○ Edit

○ SEO

Keyword	Tags

Content

Checklist

○ —————————

○ —————————

○ —————————

○ —————————

○ —————————

○ —————————

○ —————————

○ —————————

○ —————————

○ —————————

○ —————————

Resources

Social Media

○

○

○

○

○

BLOG POST PLANNER

Publish Date ....

Category ....

Title ....

Call to Action ....

Type

- ☐ Tutorial
- ☐ Review
- ☐ List
- ☐ Guest Post

Post status

- ◯ Draft
- ◯ Scheduled
- ◯ Published
- ◯ Edit
- ◯ SEO

Keyword	Tags

Checklist

- ◯ ————————————
- ◯ ————————————
- ◯ ————————————
- ◯ ————————————
- ◯ ————————————
- ◯ ————————————
- ◯ ————————————
- ◯ ————————————
- ◯ ————————————
- ◯ ————————————
- ◯ ————————————

Content ....

Resources

Social Media

- ◯
- ◯
- ◯
- ◯
- ◯

BLOG POST PLANNER

Publish Date

Category

Title

Call to Action

Type

☐ Tutorial   ☐ List

☐ Review   ☐ Guest Post

Post status

○ Draft

○ Scheduled

○ Published

○ Edit

○ SEO

Keyword	Tags

Checklist

Content

Resources

Social Media

BLOG POST PLANNER

Publish Date

Category

Title

Call to Action

Type

☐ Tutorial   ☐ List

☐ Review   ☐ Guest Post

Post status

○ Draft

○ Scheduled

○ Published

○ Edit

○ SEO

Keyword	Tags

Content

Checklist

○

○

○

○

○

○

○

○

○

○

○

Resources

Social Media

○

○

○

○

○

BLOG POST PLANNER

Publish Date

Category

Title

Call to Action

Type

- [ ] Tutorial
- [ ] Review
- [ ] List
- [ ] Guest Post

Post status

- ○ Draft
- ○ Scheduled
- ○ Published
- ○ Edit
- ○ SEO

Keyword	Tags

Content

Checklist

- ○
- ○
- ○
- ○
- ○
- ○
- ○
- ○
- ○
- ○
- ○

Resources

Social Media

- ○
- ○
- ○
- ○
- ○

BLOG POST PLANNER

Publish Date ....

Category ....

Title ....

Call to Action ....

Type

☐ Tutorial   ☐ List

☐ Review   ☐ Guest Post

Post status

○ Draft

○ Scheduled

○ Published

○ Edit

○ SEO

Keyword	Tags

Checklist

○ ——————————
○ ——————————
○ ——————————
○ ——————————
○ ——————————
○ ——————————
○ ——————————
○ ——————————
○ ——————————
○ ——————————
○ ——————————

Content ....

Resources

Social Media

○
○
○
○
○

BLOG POST PLANNER

Publish Date

Category

Title

Call to Action

Type

☐ Tutorial ☐ List

☐ Review ☐ Guest Post

Post status

○ Draft

○ Scheduled

○ Published

○ Edit

○ SEO

Keyword	Tags

Checklist

○ ——————————
○ ——————————
○ ——————————
○ ——————————
○ ——————————
○ ——————————
○ ——————————
○ ——————————
○ ——————————
○ ——————————
○ ——————————

Content

Resources

Social Media

○
○
○
○
○

BLOG POST PLANNER

Publish Date ....

Category ....

Title ....

Call to Action ....
....

Type

- ☐ Tutorial
- ☐ Review
- ☐ List
- ☐ Guest Post

Post status

- ○ Draft
- ○ Scheduled
- ○ Published
- ○ Edit
- ○ SEO

Keyword	Tags

Checklist

- ○ ________________
- ○ ________________
- ○ ________________
- ○ ________________
- ○ ________________
- ○ ________________
- ○ ________________
- ○ ________________
- ○ ________________
- ○ ________________
- ○ ________________

Content

Resources

Social Media

- ○
- ○
- ○
- ○
- ○

BLOG POST PLANNER

Publish Date

Category

Title

Call to Action

Type

- Tutorial
- Review
- List
- Guest Post

Post status

- Draft
- Scheduled
- Published
- Edit
- SEO

Keyword	Tags

Content

Checklist

Resources

Social Media

BLOG POST PLANNER

Publish Date

Category

Title

Call to Action

Type

☐ Tutorial ☐ List

☐ Review ☐ Guest Post

Post status

○ Draft

○ Scheduled

○ Published

○ Edit

○ SEO

Keyword	Tags

Content

Checklist

○ ———
○ ———
○ ———
○ ———
○ ———
○ ———
○ ———
○ ———
○ ———
○ ———
○ ———

Resources

Social Media

○
○
○
○
○

BLOG POST PLANNER

Publish Date ....

Category ....

Title

....

Call to Action ....

....

Type

☐ Tutorial　　　　☐ List
☐ Review　　　　☐ Guest Post

Post status

○ Draft

○ Scheduled

○ Published

○ Edit

○ SEO

Keyword	Tags

Content

....

....

....

....

Checklist

○ ————————————
○ ————————————
○ ————————————
○ ————————————
○ ————————————
○ ————————————
○ ————————————
○ ————————————
○ ————————————
○ ————————————
○ ————————————

Resources

Social Media

○

○

○

○

○

BLOG POST PLANNER

Publish Date ....

Category ....

Title ....

Call to Action ....

....

Type

- ☐ Tutorial
- ☐ Review
- ☐ List
- ☐ Guest Post

Post status

- ○ Draft
- ○ Scheduled
- ○ Published
- ○ Edit
- ○ SEO

Keyword	Tags

Content

Checklist

- ○ ————————————
- ○ ————————————
- ○ ————————————
- ○ ————————————
- ○ ————————————
- ○ ————————————
- ○ ————————————
- ○ ————————————
- ○ ————————————
- ○ ————————————
- ○ ————————————

Resources

Social Media

- ○
- ○
- ○
- ○
- ○

BLOG POST PLANNER

Publish Date

Category

Title

Call to Action

Type

- ☐ Tutorial
- ☐ Review
- ☐ List
- ☐ Guest Post

Post status

- ○ Draft
- ○ Scheduled
- ○ Published
- ○ Edit
- ○ SEO

Keyword	Tags

Content

Checklist

- ○
- ○
- ○
- ○
- ○
- ○
- ○
- ○
- ○
- ○
- ○

Resources

Social Media

- ○
- ○
- ○
- ○
- ○

BLOG POST PLANNER

Publish Date ....

Category ....

Title ....

Call to Action
....

Type

- ☐ Tutorial
- ☐ Review
- ☐ List
- ☐ Guest Post

Post status

- ○ Draft
- ○ Scheduled
- ○ Published
- ○ Edit
- ○ SEO

Keyword	Tags

Checklist

- ○ ______________
- ○ ______________
- ○ ______________
- ○ ______________
- ○ ______________
- ○ ______________
- ○ ______________
- ○ ______________
- ○ ______________
- ○ ______________
- ○ ______________

Content
....

Resources

Social Media

- ○
- ○
- ○
- ○
- ○

BLOG POST PLANNER

Publish Date

Category

Title

Call to Action

Type

☐ Tutorial ☐ List
☐ Review ☐ Guest Post

Post status

○ Draft

○ Scheduled

○ Published

○ Edit

○ SEO

Keyword	Tags

Checklist

Content

Resources

Social Media

BLOG POST PLANNER

Publish Date ....

Category ....

Title ....

Call to Action ....

....

Type

- ☐ Tutorial
- ☐ Review
- ☐ List
- ☐ Guest Post

Keyword	Tags

Content

....

....

....

....

Post status

- ○ Draft
- ○ Scheduled
- ○ Published
- ○ Edit
- ○ SEO

Checklist

- ○ ....
- ○ ....
- ○ ....
- ○ ....
- ○ ....
- ○ ....
- ○ ....
- ○ ....
- ○ ....
- ○ ....
- ○ ....

Resources

Social Media

- ○
- ○
- ○
- ○
- ○

BLOG POST PLANNER

Publish Date

Category

Title

Call to Action

Type

- ☐ Tutorial
- ☐ Review
- ☐ List
- ☐ Guest Post

Post status

- ○ Draft
- ○ Scheduled
- ○ Published
- ○ Edit
- ○ SEO

Keyword	Tags

Content

Checklist

- ○
- ○
- ○
- ○
- ○
- ○
- ○
- ○
- ○
- ○
- ○

Resources

Social Media

- ○
- ○
- ○
- ○
- ○

BLOG POST PLANNER

Publish Date

Category

Title

Call to Action

Type

☐ Tutorial   ☐ List

☐ Review   ☐ Guest Post

Post status

○ Draft

○ Scheduled

○ Published

○ Edit

○ SEO

Keyword	Tags

Checklist

○ ───────────
○ ───────────
○ ───────────
○ ───────────
○ ───────────
○ ───────────
○ ───────────
○ ───────────
○ ───────────
○ ───────────
○ ───────────

Content

Resources

Social Media

○
○
○
○
○

BLOG POST PLANNER

Publish Date

Category

Title

Call to Action

Type

☐ Tutorial ☐ List

☐ Review ☐ Guest Post

Post status

○ Draft

○ Scheduled

○ Published

○ Edit

○ SEO

Keyword	Tags

Checklist

○
○
○
○
○
○
○
○
○
○
○

Content

Resources

Social Media

○
○
○
○
○

BLOG POST PLANNER

Publish Date

Category

Title

Call to Action

Type

- ☐ Tutorial
- ☐ Review
- ☐ List
- ☐ Guest Post

Post status

- ○ Draft
- ○ Scheduled
- ○ Published
- ○ Edit
- ○ SEO

Keyword	Tags

Content

Checklist

- ○
- ○
- ○
- ○
- ○
- ○
- ○
- ○
- ○
- ○
- ○

Resources

Social Media

- ○
- ○
- ○
- ○
- ○

BLOG POST PLANNER

Publish Date

Category

Title

Call to Action

Type

- ☐ Tutorial
- ☐ Review
- ☐ List
- ☐ Guest Post

Post status

- ○ Draft
- ○ Scheduled
- ○ Published
- ○ Edit
- ○ SEO

Keyword	Tags

Checklist

- ○ ───────────
- ○ ───────────
- ○ ───────────
- ○ ───────────
- ○ ───────────
- ○ ───────────
- ○ ───────────
- ○ ───────────
- ○ ───────────
- ○ ───────────
- ○ ───────────

Content

Resources

Social Media

- ○
- ○
- ○
- ○
- ○

BLOG POST PLANNER

Publish Date

Category

Title

Call to Action

Type

- ☐ Tutorial
- ☐ Review
- ☐ List
- ☐ Guest Post

Post status

- ○ Draft
- ○ Scheduled
- ○ Published
- ○ Edit
- ○ SEO

Keyword	Tags

Content

Checklist

- ○ ─────────
- ○ ─────────
- ○ ─────────
- ○ ─────────
- ○ ─────────
- ○ ─────────
- ○ ─────────
- ○ ─────────
- ○ ─────────
- ○ ─────────
- ○ ─────────

Resources

Social Media

- ○
- ○
- ○
- ○
- ○

BLOG POST PLANNER

Publish Date

Category

Title

Call to Action

Type

- [ ] Tutorial
- [ ] Review
- [ ] List
- [ ] Guest Post

Post status

- ○ Draft
- ○ Scheduled
- ○ Published
- ○ Edit
- ○ SEO

Keyword	Tags

Content

Checklist

Resources

Social Media

BLOG POST PLANNER

Publish Date

Category

Title

Call to Action

Type

☐ Tutorial   ☐ List

☐ Review   ☐ Guest Post

Post status

○ Draft

○ Scheduled

○ Published

○ Edit

○ SEO

Keyword	Tags

Checklist

○ ──────────
○ ──────────
○ ──────────
○ ──────────
○ ──────────
○ ──────────
○ ──────────
○ ──────────
○ ──────────
○ ──────────
○ ──────────

Content

Resources

Social Media

○
○
○
○
○

BLOG POST PLANNER

Publish Date ....

Category ....

Title ....

Call to Action ....

....

Type

- ☐ Tutorial
- ☐ Review
- ☐ List
- ☐ Guest Post

Post status

- ○ Draft
- ○ Scheduled
- ○ Published
- ○ Edit
- ○ SEO

Keyword	Tags

Checklist

- ○ ____________
- ○ ____________
- ○ ____________
- ○ ____________
- ○ ____________
- ○ ____________
- ○ ____________
- ○ ____________
- ○ ____________
- ○ ____________
- ○ ____________

Content

....

....

....

Resources

Social Media

- ○
- ○
- ○
- ○
- ○

BLOG POST PLANNER

Publish Date

Category

Title

Call to Action

Type

- ☐ Tutorial
- ☐ Review
- ☐ List
- ☐ Guest Post

Post status

- ○ Draft
- ○ Scheduled
- ○ Published
- ○ Edit
- ○ SEO

Keyword	Tags

Content

Checklist

- ○
- ○
- ○
- ○
- ○
- ○
- ○
- ○
- ○
- ○
- ○

Resources

Social Media

- ○
- ○
- ○
- ○
- ○

BLOG POST PLANNER

Publish Date

Category

Title

Call to Action

Type

- ☐ Tutorial
- ☐ Review
- ☐ List
- ☐ Guest Post

Post status

- ○ Draft
- ○ Scheduled
- ○ Published
- ○ Edit
- ○ SEO

Keyword	Tags

Checklist

Content

Resources

Social Media

BLOG POST PLANNER

Publish Date ....

Category ....

Title ....

Call to Action ....

....

Type

- ☐ Tutorial
- ☐ Review
- ☐ List
- ☐ Guest Post

Post status

- ○ Draft
- ○ Scheduled
- ○ Published
- ○ Edit
- ○ SEO

Keyword	Tags

Checklist

- ○ ——————————
- ○ ——————————
- ○ ——————————
- ○ ——————————
- ○ ——————————
- ○ ——————————
- ○ ——————————
- ○ ——————————
- ○ ——————————
- ○ ——————————
- ○ ——————————

Content ....

....

....

....

Resources

Social Media

- ○
- ○
- ○
- ○
- ○

BLOG POST PLANNER

Publish Date ....

Category ....

Title ....

Call to Action ....

....

Type

- ☐ Tutorial
- ☐ Review
- ☐ List
- ☐ Guest Post

Post status

- ○ Draft
- ○ Scheduled
- ○ Published
- ○ Edit
- ○ SEO

Keyword	Tags

Content ....

....

....

....

Checklist

- ○ ——————————
- ○ ——————————
- ○ ——————————
- ○ ——————————
- ○ ——————————
- ○ ——————————
- ○ ——————————
- ○ ——————————
- ○ ——————————
- ○ ——————————
- ○ ——————————

Resources

Social Media

- ○
- ○
- ○
- ○
- ○

BLOG POST PLANNER

Publish Date

Category

Title

Call to Action

Type

☐ Tutorial   ☐ List
☐ Review   ☐ Guest Post

Post status

○ Draft
○ Scheduled
○ Published
○ Edit
○ SEO

Keyword	Tags

Checklist

○
○
○
○
○
○
○
○
○
○
○

Content

Resources

Social Media

○
○
○
○
○

BLOG POST PLANNER

Publish Date

Category

Title

Call to Action

Type

- ☐ Tutorial
- ☐ Review
- ☐ List
- ☐ Guest Post

Post status

- ○ Draft
- ○ Scheduled
- ○ Published
- ○ Edit
- ○ SEO

Keyword	Tags

Content

Checklist

- ○
- ○
- ○
- ○
- ○
- ○
- ○
- ○
- ○
- ○
- ○

Resources

Social Media

- ○
- ○
- ○
- ○
- ○

BLOG POST PLANNER

Publish Date

Category

Title

Call to Action

Type

- ☐ Tutorial
- ☐ Review
- ☐ List
- ☐ Guest Post

Post status

- ○ Draft
- ○ Scheduled
- ○ Published
- ○ Edit
- ○ SEO

Keyword	Tags

Content

Checklist

- ○
- ○
- ○
- ○
- ○
- ○
- ○
- ○
- ○
- ○
- ○

Resources

Social Media

- ○
- ○
- ○
- ○
- ○

BLOG POST PLANNER

Publish Date

Category

Title

Call to Action

Type

- ☐ Tutorial
- ☐ Review
- ☐ List
- ☐ Guest Post

Post status

- ○ Draft
- ○ Scheduled
- ○ Published
- ○ Edit
- ○ SEO

Keyword	Tags

Content

Checklist

- ○
- ○
- ○
- ○
- ○
- ○
- ○
- ○
- ○
- ○
- ○

Resources

Social Media

- ○
- ○
- ○
- ○
- ○

BLOG POST PLANNER

Publish Date

Category

Title

Call to Action

Type

☐ Tutorial
☐ Review

☐ List
☐ Guest Post

Post status

○ Draft

○ Scheduled

○ Published

○ Edit

○ SEO

Keyword	Tags

Content

Checklist

○ ———————
○ ———————
○ ———————
○ ———————
○ ———————
○ ———————
○ ———————
○ ———————
○ ———————
○ ———————
○ ———————

Resources

Social Media

○
○
○
○
○

BLOG POST PLANNER

Publish Date ....

Category ....

Title ....

Call to Action ....

....

Type

☐ Tutorial   ☐ List

☐ Review   ☐ Guest Post

Post status

○ Draft

○ Scheduled

○ Published

○ Edit

○ SEO

Keyword	Tags

Checklist

○ ————————————
○ ————————————
○ ————————————
○ ————————————
○ ————————————
○ ————————————
○ ————————————
○ ————————————
○ ————————————
○ ————————————

Content ....

Resources

Social Media

○

○

○

○

○

BLOG POST PLANNER

Publish Date

Category

Title

Call to Action

Type

- ☐ Tutorial
- ☐ Review
- ☐ List
- ☐ Guest Post

Post status

- ○ Draft
- ○ Scheduled
- ○ Published
- ○ Edit
- ○ SEO

Keyword	Tags

Content

Checklist

- ○
- ○
- ○
- ○
- ○
- ○
- ○
- ○
- ○
- ○
- ○

Resources

Social Media

- ○
- ○
- ○
- ○
- ○

BLOG POST PLANNER

Publish Date

Category

Title

Call to Action

Type

- ☐ Tutorial
- ☐ Review
- ☐ List
- ☐ Guest Post

Post status

- ○ Draft
- ○ Scheduled
- ○ Published
- ○ Edit
- ○ SEO

Keyword	Tags

Content

Checklist

- ○
- ○
- ○
- ○
- ○
- ○
- ○
- ○
- ○
- ○
- ○

Resources

Social Media

- ○
- ○
- ○
- ○
- ○

BLOG POST PLANNER

Publish Date

Category

Title

Call to Action

Type

☐ Tutorial ☐ List

☐ Review ☐ Guest Post

Post status

○ Draft

○ Scheduled

○ Published

○ Edit

○ SEO

Keyword	Tags

Content

Checklist

○ ───────────
○ ───────────
○ ───────────
○ ───────────
○ ───────────
○ ───────────
○ ───────────
○ ───────────
○ ───────────
○ ───────────
○ ───────────

Resources

Social Media

○
○
○
○
○

BLOG POST PLANNER

Publish Date

Category

Title

Call to Action

Type

- ☐ Tutorial
- ☐ Review
- ☐ List
- ☐ Guest Post

Post status

- ○ Draft
- ○ Scheduled
- ○ Published
- ○ Edit
- ○ SEO

Keyword	Tags

Checklist

- ○ —————————————
- ○ —————————————
- ○ —————————————
- ○ —————————————
- ○ —————————————
- ○ —————————————
- ○ —————————————
- ○ —————————————
- ○ —————————————
- ○ —————————————
- ○ —————————————

Content

Resources

Social Media

- ○
- ○
- ○
- ○
- ○

BLOG POST PLANNER

Publish Date

Category

Title

Call to Action

Type

- ☐ Tutorial
- ☐ Review
- ☐ List
- ☐ Guest Post

Post status

- ○ Draft
- ○ Scheduled
- ○ Published
- ○ Edit
- ○ SEO

Keyword	Tags

Content

Checklist

- ○ ———
- ○ ———
- ○ ———
- ○ ———
- ○ ———
- ○ ———
- ○ ———
- ○ ———
- ○ ———
- ○ ———
- ○ ———

Resources

Social Media

- ○
- ○
- ○
- ○
- ○

BLOG POST PLANNER

Publish Date

Category

Title

Call to Action

Type

- ☐ Tutorial
- ☐ Review
- ☐ List
- ☐ Guest Post

Post status

- ○ Draft
- ○ Scheduled
- ○ Published
- ○ Edit
- ○ SEO

Keyword	Tags

Content

Checklist

- ○
- ○
- ○
- ○
- ○
- ○
- ○
- ○
- ○
- ○
- ○

Resources

Social Media

- ○
- ○
- ○
- ○
- ○

BLOG POST PLANNER

Publish Date ....

Category ....

Title ....

Call to Action ....

Type

☐ Tutorial   ☐ List
☐ Review   ☐ Guest Post

Post status

○ Draft

○ Scheduled

○ Published

○ Edit

○ SEO

Keyword	Tags

Checklist

○ ____________
○ ____________
○ ____________
○ ____________
○ ____________
○ ____________
○ ____________
○ ____________
○ ____________
○ ____________
○ ____________

Content ....

Resources

Social Media

○
○
○
○
○

BLOG POST PLANNER

Publish Date

Category

Title

Call to Action

Type

☐ Tutorial ☐ List

☐ Review ☐ Guest Post

Post status

○ Draft

○ Scheduled

○ Published

○ Edit

○ SEO

Keyword	Tags

Content

Checklist

○ ──────────
○ ──────────
○ ──────────
○ ──────────
○ ──────────
○ ──────────
○ ──────────
○ ──────────
○ ──────────
○ ──────────
○ ──────────

Resources

Social Media

○
○
○
○
○

BLOG POST PLANNER

Publish Date

Category

Title

Call to Action

Type

- ☐ Tutorial
- ☐ Review
- ☐ List
- ☐ Guest Post

Post status

- ○ Draft
- ○ Scheduled
- ○ Published
- ○ Edit
- ○ SEO

Keyword	Tags

Content

Checklist

- ○
- ○
- ○
- ○
- ○
- ○
- ○
- ○
- ○
- ○
- ○

Resources

Social Media

- ○
- ○
- ○
- ○
- ○

BLOG POST PLANNER

Publish Date

Category

Title

Call to Action

Type

☐ Tutorial   ☐ List

☐ Review   ☐ Guest Post

Post status

○ Draft

○ Scheduled

○ Published

○ Edit

○ SEO

Keyword	Tags

Checklist

Content

Resources

Social Media

BLOG POST PLANNER

Publish Date ....

Category ....

Title ....

Call to Action ....

Type

- ☐ Tutorial
- ☐ Review
- ☐ List
- ☐ Guest Post

Post status

- ○ Draft
- ○ Scheduled
- ○ Published
- ○ Edit
- ○ SEO

Keyword	Tags

Checklist

- ○ ________________
- ○ ________________
- ○ ________________
- ○ ________________
- ○ ________________
- ○ ________________
- ○ ________________
- ○ ________________
- ○ ________________
- ○ ________________
- ○ ________________

Content

....

Resources

Social Media

- ○
- ○
- ○
- ○
- ○

BLOG POST PLANNER

Publish Date

Category

Title

Call to Action

Type

- ☐ Tutorial
- ☐ Review
- ☐ List
- ☐ Guest Post

Post status

- ○ Draft
- ○ Scheduled
- ○ Published
- ○ Edit
- ○ SEO

Keyword	Tags

Checklist

Content

Resources

Social Media

BLOG POST PLANNER

Publish Date ....

Category ....

Title ....

Call to Action ....

Type

☐ Tutorial   ☐ List

☐ Review   ☐ Guest Post

Post status

○ Draft

○ Scheduled

○ Published

○ Edit

○ SEO

Keyword	Tags

Content

....

Checklist

○ —————————————

○ —————————————

○ —————————————

○ —————————————

○ —————————————

○ —————————————

○ —————————————

○ —————————————

○ —————————————

○ —————————————

Resources

Social Media

○

○

○

○

○

BLOG POST PLANNER

Publish Date

Category

Title

Call to Action

Type

- [ ] Tutorial
- [ ] List
- [ ] Review
- [ ] Guest Post

Post status

- ○ Draft
- ○ Scheduled
- ○ Published
- ○ Edit
- ○ SEO

Keyword	Tags

Checklist

Content

Resources

Social Media

BLOG POST PLANNER

Publish Date

Category

Title

Call to Action

Type

- ☐ Tutorial
- ☐ Review
- ☐ List
- ☐ Guest Post

Post status

- ○ Draft
- ○ Scheduled
- ○ Published
- ○ Edit
- ○ SEO

Keyword	Tags

Content

Checklist

- ○
- ○
- ○
- ○
- ○
- ○
- ○
- ○
- ○
- ○
- ○

Resources

Social Media

- ○
- ○
- ○
- ○
- ○

BLOG POST PLANNER

Publish Date

Category

Title

Call to Action

Type

- ☐ Tutorial
- ☐ Review
- ☐ List
- ☐ Guest Post

Post status

- ○ Draft
- ○ Scheduled
- ○ Published
- ○ Edit
- ○ SEO

Keyword	Tags

Content

Checklist

- ○ _______________
- ○ _______________
- ○ _______________
- ○ _______________
- ○ _______________
- ○ _______________
- ○ _______________
- ○ _______________
- ○ _______________
- ○ _______________
- ○ _______________

Resources

Social Media

- ○
- ○
- ○
- ○
- ○

BLOG POST PLANNER

Publish Date

Category

Title

Call to Action

Type

- Tutorial
- Review
- List
- Guest Post

Post status

- Draft
- Scheduled
- Published
- Edit
- SEO

Keyword	Tags

Checklist

Content

Resources

Social Media

BLOG POST PLANNER

Publish Date ....

Category ....

Title ....

Call to Action ....
....

Type

- ☐ Tutorial
- ☐ Review
- ☐ List
- ☐ Guest Post

Post status

- ○ Draft
- ○ Scheduled
- ○ Published
- ○ Edit
- ○ SEO

Keyword	Tags

Content ....

Checklist

- ○ ________________
- ○ ________________
- ○ ________________
- ○ ________________
- ○ ________________
- ○ ________________
- ○ ________________
- ○ ________________
- ○ ________________
- ○ ________________
- ○ ________________

Resources

Social Media

- ○
- ○
- ○
- ○
- ○

BLOG POST PLANNER

Publish Date

Category

Title

Call to Action

Type

- ☐ Tutorial
- ☐ Review
- ☐ List
- ☐ Guest Post

Post status

- ○ Draft
- ○ Scheduled
- ○ Published
- ○ Edit
- ○ SEO

Keyword	Tags

Content

Checklist

- ○
- ○
- ○
- ○
- ○
- ○
- ○
- ○
- ○
- ○
- ○

Resources

Social Media

- ○
- ○
- ○
- ○
- ○

BLOG POST PLANNER

Publish Date

Category

Title

Call to Action

Type

- [ ] Tutorial
- [ ] Review
- [ ] List
- [ ] Guest Post

Post status

- ○ Draft
- ○ Scheduled
- ○ Published
- ○ Edit
- ○ SEO

Keyword	Tags

Content

Checklist

Resources

Social Media

BLOG POST PLANNER

Publish Date

Category

Title

Call to Action

Type

☐ Tutorial   ☐ List

☐ Review   ☐ Guest Post

Post status

○ Draft

○ Scheduled

○ Published

○ Edit

○ SEO

Keyword	Tags

Checklist

○ ————————————

○ ————————————

○ ————————————

○ ————————————

○ ————————————

○ ————————————

○ ————————————

○ ————————————

○ ————————————

○ ————————————

○ ————————————

Content

Resources

Social Media

○

○

○

○

○

BLOG POST PLANNER

Publish Date

Category

Title

Call to Action

Type

- ☐ Tutorial
- ☐ Review
- ☐ List
- ☐ Guest Post

Post status

- ○ Draft
- ○ Scheduled
- ○ Published
- ○ Edit
- ○ SEO

Keyword	Tags

Checklist

- ○
- ○
- ○
- ○
- ○
- ○
- ○
- ○
- ○
- ○
- ○

Content

Resources

Social Media

- ○
- ○
- ○
- ○
- ○

BLOG POST PLANNER

Publish Date ....

Category ....

Title ....

Call to Action ....

Type

- [ ] Tutorial
- [ ] Review
- [ ] List
- [ ] Guest Post

Post status

- ○ Draft
- ○ Scheduled
- ○ Published
- ○ Edit
- ○ SEO

Keyword	Tags

Checklist

- ○ ____________________
- ○ ____________________
- ○ ____________________
- ○ ____________________
- ○ ____________________
- ○ ____________________
- ○ ____________________
- ○ ____________________
- ○ ____________________
- ○ ____________________
- ○ ____________________

Content

Resources

Social Media

- ○
- ○
- ○
- ○
- ○

BLOG POST PLANNER

Publish Date ....

Category ....

Title ....

Call to Action ....

....

Type

☐ Tutorial   ☐ List

☐ Review   ☐ Guest Post

Post status

○ Draft

○ Scheduled

○ Published

○ Edit

○ SEO

Keyword	Tags

Checklist

○ ——————————————

○ ——————————————

○ ——————————————

○ ——————————————

○ ——————————————

○ ——————————————

○ ——————————————

○ ——————————————

○ ——————————————

○ ——————————————

○ ——————————————

Content

....

....

....

Resources

Social Media

○

○

○

○

○

BLOG POST PLANNER

Publish Date

Category

Title

Call to Action

Type

☐ Tutorial   ☐ List
☐ Review   ☐ Guest Post

Post status

○ Draft

○ Scheduled

○ Published

○ Edit

○ SEO

Keyword	Tags

Content

Checklist

○ ———————————
○ ———————————
○ ———————————
○ ———————————
○ ———————————
○ ———————————
○ ———————————
○ ———————————
○ ———————————
○ ———————————
○ ———————————

Resources

Social Media

○

○

○

○

○

BLOG POST PLANNER

Publish Date

Category

Title

Call to Action

Type

- Tutorial
- Review
- List
- Guest Post

Post status

- ○ Draft
- ○ Scheduled
- ○ Published
- ○ Edit
- ○ SEO

Keyword	Tags

Checklist

- ○
- ○
- ○
- ○
- ○
- ○
- ○
- ○
- ○
- ○
- ○

Content

Resources

Social Media

- ○
- ○
- ○
- ○
- ○

BLOG POST PLANNER

Publish Date ....

Category ....

Title ....

Call to Action ....

....

Type

☐ Tutorial   ☐ List

☐ Review   ☐ Guest Post

Post status

○ Draft

○ Scheduled

○ Published

○ Edit

○ SEO

Keyword	Tags

Checklist

○ ——————————————

○ ——————————————

○ ——————————————

○ ——————————————

○ ——————————————

○ ——————————————

○ ——————————————

○ ——————————————

○ ——————————————

○ ——————————————

○ ——————————————

Content

....

....

....

....

Resources

Social Media

○

○

○

○

○

BLOG POST PLANNER

Publish Date ....

Category ....

Title ....

Call to Action ....

....

Type

☐ Tutorial   ☐ List

☐ Review   ☐ Guest Post

Post status

○ Draft

○ Scheduled

○ Published

○ Edit

○ SEO

Keyword	Tags

Checklist

○ ________________________

○ ________________________

○ ________________________

○ ________________________

○ ________________________

○ ________________________

○ ________________________

○ ________________________

○ ________________________

○ ________________________

○ ________________________

Content

....

....

....

Resources

Social Media

○

○

○

○

○

BLOG POST PLANNER

Publish Date

Category

Title

Call to Action

Type

☐ Tutorial ☐ List

☐ Review ☐ Guest Post

Post status

○ Draft

○ Scheduled

○ Published

○ Edit

○ SEO

Keyword	Tags

Checklist

○ —————

○ —————

○ —————

○ —————

○ —————

○ —————

○ —————

○ —————

○ —————

○ —————

○ —————

Content

Resources

Social Media

○

○

○

○

○

BLOG POST PLANNER

Publish Date

Category

Title

Call to Action

Type

☐ Tutorial ☐ List

☐ Review ☐ Guest Post

Post status

○ Draft

○ Scheduled

○ Published

○ Edit

○ SEO

Keyword	Tags

Content

Checklist

Resources

Social Media

BLOG POST PLANNER

Publish Date ....

Category ....

Title ....

Call to Action ....
....

Type

☐ Tutorial ☐ List

☐ Review ☐ Guest Post

Post status

○ Draft

○ Scheduled

○ Published

○ Edit

○ SEO

Keyword	Tags

Checklist

○ ———————————————

○ ———————————————

○ ———————————————

○ ———————————————

○ ———————————————

○ ———————————————

○ ———————————————

○ ———————————————

○ ———————————————

○ ———————————————

○ ———————————————

Content ....
....
....
....

Resources

Social Media

○

○

○

○

○

BLOG POST PLANNER

Publish Date

Category

Title

Call to Action

Type

- ☐ Tutorial
- ☐ Review
- ☐ List
- ☐ Guest Post

Post status

- ○ Draft
- ○ Scheduled
- ○ Published
- ○ Edit
- ○ SEO

Keyword	Tags

Content

Checklist

- ○
- ○
- ○
- ○
- ○
- ○
- ○
- ○
- ○
- ○
- ○

Resources

Social Media

- ○
- ○
- ○
- ○
- ○

BLOG POST PLANNER

Publish Date ___________________

Category ___________________

Title ___________________

Call to Action ___________________

Type

- ☐ Tutorial
- ☐ Review
- ☐ List
- ☐ Guest Post

Post status

- ○ Draft
- ○ Scheduled
- ○ Published
- ○ Edit
- ○ SEO

Keyword	Tags

Content

Checklist

- ○ ___________________
- ○ ___________________
- ○ ___________________
- ○ ___________________
- ○ ___________________
- ○ ___________________
- ○ ___________________
- ○ ___________________
- ○ ___________________
- ○ ___________________
- ○ ___________________

Resources

Social Media

- ○
- ○
- ○
- ○
- ○

BLOG POST PLANNER

Publish Date ....

Category ....

Title ....

Call to Action

....

Type

- ☐ Tutorial
- ☐ List
- ☐ Review
- ☐ Guest Post

Post status

- ○ Draft
- ○ Scheduled
- ○ Published
- ○ Edit
- ○ SEO

Keyword	Tags

Content

....

Checklist

- ○ ——————
- ○ ——————
- ○ ——————
- ○ ——————
- ○ ——————
- ○ ——————
- ○ ——————
- ○ ——————
- ○ ——————
- ○ ——————
- ○ ——————

Resources

Social Media

- ○
- ○
- ○
- ○
- ○

BLOG POST PLANNER

Publish Date

Category

Title

Call to Action

Type

☐ Tutorial

☐ Review

☐ List

☐ Guest Post

Post status

○ Draft

○ Scheduled

○ Published

○ Edit

○ SEO

Keyword	Tags

Checklist

○ ————————————

○ ————————————

○ ————————————

○ ————————————

○ ————————————

○ ————————————

○ ————————————

○ ————————————

○ ————————————

○ ————————————

○ ————————————

Content

Resources

Social Media

○

○

○

○

○

BLOG POST PLANNER

Publish Date

Category

Title

Call to Action

Type

☐ Tutorial

☐ Review

☐ List

☐ Guest Post

Post status

○ Draft

○ Scheduled

○ Published

○ Edit

○ SEO

Keyword	Tags

Content

Checklist

○

○

○

○

○

○

○

○

○

○

○

Resources

Social Media

○

○

○

○

○

BLOG POST PLANNER

Publish Date ....

Category ....

Title ....

Call to Action ....

Type

- ☐ Tutorial
- ☐ Review
- ☐ List
- ☐ Guest Post

Post status

- ○ Draft
- ○ Scheduled
- ○ Published
- ○ Edit
- ○ SEO

Keyword	Tags

Checklist

- ○ —————————————
- ○ —————————————
- ○ —————————————
- ○ —————————————
- ○ —————————————
- ○ —————————————
- ○ —————————————
- ○ —————————————
- ○ —————————————
- ○ —————————————
- ○ —————————————

Content

....

....

....

Resources

Social Media

- ○
- ○
- ○
- ○
- ○

BLOG POST PLANNER

Publish Date ....

Category ....

Title ....

Call to Action ....

Type

- ☐ Tutorial
- ☐ Review
- ☐ List
- ☐ Guest Post

Post status

- ○ Draft
- ○ Scheduled
- ○ Published
- ○ Edit
- ○ SEO

Keyword	Tags

Checklist

- ○ ——————————
- ○ ——————————
- ○ ——————————
- ○ ——————————
- ○ ——————————
- ○ ——————————
- ○ ——————————
- ○ ——————————
- ○ ——————————
- ○ ——————————
- ○ ——————————

Content ....

Resources

Social Media

- ○
- ○
- ○
- ○
- ○

BLOG POST PLANNER

Publish Date ....

Category ....

Title ....

Call to Action ....

Type

☐ Tutorial ☐ List

☐ Review ☐ Guest Post

Post status

○ Draft

○ Scheduled

○ Published

○ Edit

○ SEO

Keyword	Tags

Checklist

○ —————————————
○ —————————————
○ —————————————
○ —————————————
○ —————————————
○ —————————————
○ —————————————
○ —————————————
○ —————————————
○ —————————————
○ —————————————

Content ....

Resources

Social Media

○

○

○

○

○

BLOG POST PLANNER

Publish Date

Category

Title

Call to Action

Type

☐ Tutorial   ☐ List

☐ Review   ☐ Guest Post

Post status

○ Draft

○ Scheduled

○ Published

○ Edit

○ SEO

Keyword	Tags

Checklist

○ ——————————
○ ——————————
○ ——————————
○ ——————————
○ ——————————
○ ——————————
○ ——————————
○ ——————————
○ ——————————
○ ——————————
○ ——————————

Content

Resources

Social Media

○

○

○

○

○

BLOG POST PLANNER

Publish Date ....

Category ....

Title ....

Call to Action ....

....

Type

- [ ] Tutorial
- [ ] Review
- [ ] List
- [ ] Guest Post

Post status

- ○ Draft
- ○ Scheduled
- ○ Published
- ○ Edit
- ○ SEO

Keyword	Tags

Content ....

....

....

....

Checklist

- ○ ________________
- ○ ________________
- ○ ________________
- ○ ________________
- ○ ________________
- ○ ________________
- ○ ________________
- ○ ________________
- ○ ________________
- ○ ________________
- ○ ________________

Resources

Social Media

- ○
- ○
- ○
- ○
- ○

BLOG POST PLANNER

Publish Date

Category

Title

Call to Action

Type

☐ Tutorial
☐ Review

☐ List
☐ Guest Post

Post status

○ Draft

○ Scheduled

○ Published

○ Edit

○ SEO

Keyword	Tags

Checklist

○
○
○
○
○
○
○
○
○
○
○

Content

Resources

Social Media

○
○
○
○
○

BLOG POST PLANNER

Publish Date

Category

Title

Call to Action

Type

- ☐ Tutorial
- ☐ Review
- ☐ List
- ☐ Guest Post

Post status

- ○ Draft
- ○ Scheduled
- ○ Published
- ○ Edit
- ○ SEO

Keyword	Tags

Checklist

- ○
- ○
- ○
- ○
- ○
- ○
- ○
- ○
- ○
- ○
- ○

Content

Resources

Social Media

- ○
- ○
- ○
- ○
- ○

BLOG POST PLANNER

Publish Date

Category

Title

Call to Action

Type

- ☐ Tutorial
- ☐ Review
- ☐ List
- ☐ Guest Post

Post status

- ○ Draft
- ○ Scheduled
- ○ Published
- ○ Edit
- ○ SEO

Keyword	Tags

Checklist

- ○
- ○
- ○
- ○
- ○
- ○
- ○
- ○
- ○
- ○
- ○

Content

Resources

Social Media

- ○
- ○
- ○
- ○
- ○

BLOG POST PLANNER

Publish Date

Category

Title

Call to Action

Type

- ☐ Tutorial
- ☐ Review
- ☐ List
- ☐ Guest Post

Post status

- ○ Draft
- ○ Scheduled
- ○ Published
- ○ Edit
- ○ SEO

Keyword	Tags

Checklist

- ○
- ○
- ○
- ○
- ○
- ○
- ○
- ○
- ○
- ○
- ○

Content

Resources

Social Media

- ○
- ○
- ○
- ○
- ○

BLOG POST PLANNER

Publish Date

Category

Title

Call to Action

Type

- ☐ Tutorial
- ☐ Review
- ☐ List
- ☐ Guest Post

Post status

- ○ Draft
- ○ Scheduled
- ○ Published
- ○ Edit
- ○ SEO

Keyword	Tags

Content

Checklist

- ○ —
- ○ —
- ○ —
- ○ —
- ○ —
- ○ —
- ○ —
- ○ —
- ○ —
- ○ —

Resources

Social Media

- ○
- ○
- ○
- ○
- ○

BLOG POST PLANNER

Publish Date ....

Category ....

Title ....

Call to Action ....

Type

- ☐ Tutorial
- ☐ Review
- ☐ List
- ☐ Guest Post

Post status

- ○ Draft
- ○ Scheduled
- ○ Published
- ○ Edit
- ○ SEO

Keyword	Tags

Checklist

- ○ ________________
- ○ ________________
- ○ ________________
- ○ ________________
- ○ ________________
- ○ ________________
- ○ ________________
- ○ ________________
- ○ ________________
- ○ ________________
- ○ ________________

Content

Resources

Social Media

- ○
- ○
- ○
- ○
- ○

BLOG POST PLANNER

Publish Date

Category

Title

Call to Action

Type

☐ Tutorial ☐ List

☐ Review ☐ Guest Post

Post status

○ Draft

○ Scheduled

○ Published

○ Edit

○ SEO

Keyword	Tags

Checklist

○ —————————————
○ —————————————
○ —————————————
○ —————————————
○ —————————————
○ —————————————
○ —————————————
○ —————————————
○ —————————————
○ —————————————
○ —————————————

Content

Resources

Social Media

○

○

○

○

○

BLOG POST PLANNER

Publish Date

Category

Title

Call to Action

Type

☐ Tutorial   ☐ List

☐ Review   ☐ Guest Post

Post status

○ Draft

○ Scheduled

○ Published

○ Edit

○ SEO

Keyword	Tags

Checklist

○ ──────────
○ ──────────
○ ──────────
○ ──────────
○ ──────────
○ ──────────
○ ──────────
○ ──────────
○ ──────────
○ ──────────
○ ──────────

Content

Resources

Social Media

○

○

○

○

○

BLOG POST PLANNER

Publish Date

Category

Title

Call to Action

Type

☐ Tutorial ☐ List
☐ Review ☐ Guest Post

Post status

○ Draft
○ Scheduled
○ Published
○ Edit
○ SEO

Keyword	Tags

Content

Checklist

○ ————————
○ ————————
○ ————————
○ ————————
○ ————————
○ ————————
○ ————————
○ ————————
○ ————————
○ ————————
○ ————————

Resources

Social Media

○
○
○
○
○

BLOG POST PLANNER

Publish Date

Category

Title

Call to Action

Type

- ☐ Tutorial
- ☐ Review
- ☐ List
- ☐ Guest Post

Post status

- ○ Draft
- ○ Scheduled
- ○ Published
- ○ Edit
- ○ SEO

Keyword	Tags

Content

Checklist

- ○ ______
- ○ ______
- ○ ______
- ○ ______
- ○ ______
- ○ ______
- ○ ______
- ○ ______
- ○ ______
- ○ ______
- ○ ______

Resources

Social Media

- ○
- ○
- ○
- ○
- ○

BLOG POST PLANNER

Publish Date

Category

Title

Call to Action

Type

☐ Tutorial　　☐ List
☐ Review　　☐ Guest Post

Post status

○ Draft

○ Scheduled

○ Published

○ Edit

○ SEO

Keyword	Tags

Content

Checklist

Resources

Social Media

BLOG POST PLANNER

Publish Date ....

Category ....

Title ....

Call to Action ....

Type

- ☐ Tutorial
- ☐ Review
- ☐ List
- ☐ Guest Post

Post status

- ○ Draft
- ○ Scheduled
- ○ Published
- ○ Edit
- ○ SEO

Keyword	Tags

Content

Checklist

- ○ ————————————————
- ○ ————————————————
- ○ ————————————————
- ○ ————————————————
- ○ ————————————————
- ○ ————————————————
- ○ ————————————————
- ○ ————————————————
- ○ ————————————————
- ○ ————————————————
- ○ ————————————————

Resources

Social Media

- ○
- ○
- ○
- ○
- ○

BLOG POST PLANNER

Publish Date

Category

Title

Call to Action

Type

- ☐ Tutorial
- ☐ Review
- ☐ List
- ☐ Guest Post

Post status

- ○ Draft
- ○ Scheduled
- ○ Published
- ○ Edit
- ○ SEO

Keyword	Tags

Content

Checklist

- ○ —————
- ○ —————
- ○ —————
- ○ —————
- ○ —————
- ○ —————
- ○ —————
- ○ —————
- ○ —————
- ○ —————
- ○ —————

Resources

Social Media

- ○
- ○
- ○
- ○
- ○

BLOG POST PLANNER

Publish Date

Category

Title

Call to Action

Type

☐ Tutorial   ☐ List
☐ Review   ☐ Guest Post

Post status

○ Draft

○ Scheduled

○ Published

○ Edit

○ SEO

Keyword	Tags

Checklist

○ ——————————
○ ——————————
○ ——————————
○ ——————————
○ ——————————
○ ——————————
○ ——————————
○ ——————————
○ ——————————
○ ——————————
○ ——————————

Content

Resources

Social Media

○
○
○
○
○

BLOG POST PLANNER

Publish Date ....

Category ....

Title ....

Call to Action ....

....

Type

☐ Tutorial ☐ List

☐ Review ☐ Guest Post

Post status

○ Draft

○ Scheduled

○ Published

○ Edit

○ SEO

Keyword	Tags

Checklist

○ ————————

○ ————————

○ ————————

○ ————————

○ ————————

○ ————————

○ ————————

○ ————————

○ ————————

○ ————————

○ ————————

Content ....

....

....

....

Resources

Social Media

○

○

○

○

○

BLOG POST PLANNER

Publish Date ....

Category ....

Title ....

Call to Action ....

....

Type

☐ Tutorial   ☐ List

☐ Review   ☐ Guest Post

Post status

○ Draft

○ Scheduled

○ Published

○ Edit

○ SEO

Keyword	Tags

Checklist

○ ——————————

○ ——————————

○ ——————————

○ ——————————

○ ——————————

○ ——————————

○ ——————————

○ ——————————

○ ——————————

○ ——————————

○ ——————————

Content

Resources

Social Media

○

○

○

○

○

BLOG POST PLANNER

Publish Date

Category

Title

Call to Action

Type

- [ ] Tutorial
- [ ] Review
- [ ] List
- [ ] Guest Post

Post status

- ○ Draft
- ○ Scheduled
- ○ Published
- ○ Edit
- ○ SEO

Keyword	Tags

Content

Checklist

- ○
- ○
- ○
- ○
- ○
- ○
- ○
- ○
- ○
- ○

Resources

Social Media

- ○
- ○
- ○
- ○
- ○

BLOG POST PLANNER

Publish Date
Category

Title

Call to Action

Type

☐ Tutorial   ☐ List
☐ Review   ☐ Guest Post

Post status

○ Draft
○ Scheduled
○ Published
○ Edit
○ SEO

Keyword	Tags

Content

Checklist

Resources

Social Media

BLOG POST PLANNER

Publish Date ....

Category ....

Title ....

Call to Action ....

....

Type

- ☐ Tutorial
- ☐ Review
- ☐ List
- ☐ Guest Post

Post status

- ○ Draft
- ○ Scheduled
- ○ Published
- ○ Edit
- ○ SEO

Keyword	Tags

Checklist

- ○ ___________
- ○ ___________
- ○ ___________
- ○ ___________
- ○ ___________
- ○ ___________
- ○ ___________
- ○ ___________
- ○ ___________
- ○ ___________
- ○ ___________

Content ....

....

....

....

Resources

Social Media

- ○
- ○
- ○
- ○
- ○

www.ingramcontent.com/pod-product-compliance
Lightning Source LLC
Chambersburg PA
CBHW040144110726
48005CB00018B/2639